UNDERSTANDING YOU

Stacy-Lynn

authorHOUSE®

AuthorHouse™
1663 Liberty Drive
Bloomington, IN 47403
www.authorhouse.com
Phone: 1-800-839-8640

First published by AuthorHouse   2/9/2011

ISBN: 978-1-4567-1833-6 (sc)
ISBN: 978-1-4567-1834-3 (e)

Library of Congress Control Number: 2011901341

Printed in the United States of America

For Scott, Sylor and Susan

CONTENTS

Thank you	1
The Process of Understanding You	5
Step One: The Mirror	9
Step Two: Life Map	17
Step Three: Intentions	29
Step Four: Forgiveness	37
Step Six: Dream Interpretation, Meditation and Signs	49
Dream Interpretation	49
Meditation	53
Signs	57
Step Seven: New Beginning	61
Understanding You - Workbook	63
Step One: The Mirror	65
Step Two: Life Map	77
Step Three: Intentions	87
Step Four: Forgiveness	97
Step Five: Spirit Guide	105
Step Six: Dream Interpretation, Meditation and Signs	117
Dream Interpretation	117
Meditation	125
Signs	137
Step Seven: New Beginning	147

Thank you

First and foremost thank you for starting this journey for yourself and having faith that the words of this book will inspire you to make the changes in your life that will actually make a difference. You may have been searching and searching for something yet you are not really sure what you are searching for. All you know is that something is missing. Something is not right. Something has got to change. I know exactly what you mean and how you feel. I have been lucky enough to find these answers and it is now time for me to share them with you. This book walks you through the steps to understanding and enlightenment. The steps I go over are the steps that I myself was guided through when I reached a point in my life when things needed to change or I was not sure what would happen next. I just knew the next step was not going to be good. This process of understanding you has seven steps. The first half of the book I will walk you through the steps while letting you know some of my own struggles. The second half of the book is simply just the seven steps. I wrote the book this way so you can use my life struggles as a guide to help you understand the process. Once you are in the process and have completed reading the book you can use the second half as a reference for your journey. There are pages to journal and keep notes. Use this book to the fullest. Use this book as a tool and support. If you dedicate the time to actually going through this process you will change everything about yourself and your life. It is amazing. I have also created a website for this book www.ahigherenergy.net . The website is set up in an easy to follow format that goes right along with this book. Please visit the site.

The ultimate goal of the process and this book is to guide you on how to vibrate at "A Higher Energy". A higher energy is what each and every one of us is born with. It is the Divine energy that vibrates within each and every living thing. When we are born into this world the only energy we vibrate at is "A Higher Energy". If you look at the children of the world you will see that they view themselves, the world and all the souls that reside here in a totally different way. When a child is small they see the world as the magical place that it really is. They do not have the burden of life weighing down on them. It is not until they start to experience hardship, frustration and hate for the things in the world does their higher energy begin to slow. In order to begin to vibrate at a higher energy again you must let go of all the hardship, frustration and hate. This higher energy will make you have true understanding of your life path. It will also allow you to have appreciation for all your struggles you have gone through. You will have appreciation because you will understand if you did not go through times of struggle you would not have learned what you needed to learn in order to evolve your soul. Every trying experience we have yield a very important life lesson that we need to learn in order to evolve our souls. We evolve our soul in order to become closer to the Higher Power. My Higher Power is God. Though your name may be different the Higher Power is still the same for all of us. An almighty being that we worship and look upon for salvation. Whether your Higher Power is Mother Nature, Allah or God it does not matter, that is only the name not the meaning. As you read through the pages of my book you will uncover my life journey and the lessons I have learned. Through my lessons you will see a glimpse of yourself and what you have gone through in your life. You will be able to use my words to decode your own experiences and what they mean and why they happen in your life. All the negativity and all the self abuse you put yourself through will make sense. By realizing there are lessons will help you understand why a negative situation is occurring and help you learn your lesson faster instead of finding yourself in the same situation over and over again. This can truly be harmful to someone's self esteem, spirit and overall well being. I want to show you that we have help here throughout our lives. We have Spirit Guides that are always with us. We have passed over loved ones that continue to love us even in death. I will show you how to create your own Life Map to understand why the same situations, just with different people keep presenting its self. I will show you everything I have learned since my spiritual journey of self healing has begun.

Throughout our lives we all go through many challenging situations that have dictated our reality. We allow ourselves to be the victim of our past which in turn creates our present and our future. I am able to help you uncover why. This seven step program I have designed is the same process that I have guided many individuals through, including myself, to help them become a leader of their own life. This information I am sharing really is life changing. It has helped me uncover why I view myself and others the way I do. Why I have gone through so many challenges in my life. It has helped me uncover all the rules I have set on myself based upon situations I have gone through. It has answered the question so many people ask themselves, "Why does this keep happening to me?" It has taught me how to truly set positive intentions in every aspect of my life. It has showed me how to truly forgive someone and let go of the pain that I buried deep down into myself. It has opened my eyes to guidance I believed was always there, I was just not sure how or why to access it. It has given me an entirely new perspective on myself, my life, my relationships, my job and most importantly it has given me knowledge that I just never really had before.

The Process of Understanding You

<u>*The Mirror*</u> is the first step of the program. The Mirror process is the step of the program that helps you indentify the rules you have set on yourself. These rules are what have guided you throughout your life to get into certain situations and certain relationships. The Mirror process is ultimately a representation of your self-image. Your self-image is made up of how you view yourself physically and mentally. As we live our life we encounter many different people and experience many different events. Each person and event helps you in creating rules for yourself.

<u>*The Life Map*</u> is the second step of the program. As we go through life we experience many different situations. The Life Map will show you exactly what situations you have experienced that are lessons your soul is trying to learn. Due to the rules on your mirrors you made certain decisions to get yourself into these situations. Those life experiences on your Life Map will have either created a new rule on your mirror or re-enforced an already existing rule on your mirror from a past experience. The process of recreating your Life Map allows you to see how your mirror plays into how you make decisions in your life and it will show you what lessons your soul is trying to learn.

Intention is the third step of the program. Through this step I will guide you how to set positive intentions for yourself. Positive intentions that are re-enforced day in and day out are what will actually change a negative rule that you live your life by. If a rule on your mirror prevents you from making any type of decision for yourself or if it makes you make bad decisions in your life then that is a rule you need to change. You ultimately change that rule by setting intentions.

Forgiveness is the fourth step of the program. Forgiveness is really the ultimate key to allowing yourself to let go of the pain that you buried down into yourself. Forgiveness, true forgiveness, is a challenge but I will guide you on how to truly forgive someone.

Spirit Guides is the fifth step of the program. Spirit guides are your personal guides that you have had with you since the moment you were born in this world. They are the souls that are with you day in and day out. They are the ones that understand your mirror, your life map and they are the ones that will help you through this entire process. I will go over Spirit Guides with you and teach you how to begin to have more awareness of their existences and to begin a relationship with them.

Dream Interpretation, Meditation and Signs is the sixth step of the program. I will review with you on how to interpret your own dreams. Dreams are guidance that will help you throughout your life journey. We will go over basic mediation practices that anyone can fit into their lives. I will go over how to pay attention to signs that are all around us. If these signs are followed they will guide you throughout your life path. These signs will become very important when making major life decisions.

New Beginning is the seventh and final step of the program. Living a life vibrating at "A Higher Energy" is an amazing experience. The feeling of gratitude for everything you have in life and everything you have gone through. This is where everything ties together to have true understanding and enlightenment.

Step One: The Mirror

The first step of understanding you is called The Mirror. The Mirror process will allow you to see all of the rules you choose to live your life by. It will show you how to view your life as if you were standing in front of mirror and on that mirror you could see everything that people either told you or showed you in regards to how you will and have defined yourself in your life. The Mirror represents your self-image. This is how you truly see yourself. It may not all be bad, but the bad is what has a negative effect on your life now. It is the bad we need to either change or accept. For example, I have been called fat my entire life. When I look in the mirror of my self- image I am fat. Well, in all fairness to those that liked to point that out to me everyday throughout my life it is true. I am overweight because I do not eat healthy and exercise regularly; In fact, as I sit here writing I am enjoying a cup of tea and a few cookies. The idea that I am fat is true and it is ok. The fact that I am fat does not have to be negative it is who I am, and part of changing my self-image is accepting who I really am. If I do not want my image of myself to be overweight then I need to make changes.

I know we all want a life of true happiness. We dream about being happy. We think we are trying to be happy. Yet we constantly deny ourselves the ability to truly take control of it all. I know the reason why. We started this life as babies with the freest of all minds. We accepted everything and everyone for exactly who they were. We did not judge people on how they looked, acted or even smelled. We didn't care. We would play with anyone regardless of how much money they had or how cool they were. Now everything has changed. We have forgotten to view the world like the magical place it really is. Instead, we go through life feeling overwhelmed, stressed and full of anxiety. I know because I do it every day. I run and run around screaming at everyone around me. Thinking about how unfair it all is. Why can't I have more money and better job? Why can't I be thin and beautiful? Why when I wake up in the morning do I already have a headache? I usually began my day complaining about something.

I believe it all started when I was about 8. I was standing in the bathroom looking at myself in the mirror. I was remembering that not too long ago I was looking in this same mirror, but back then I looked totally different. Now I see that my hair is greasy and flat. My face is fat and I am anything but pretty. I am 8 years old starring at myself in the mirror, seeing my own reflection starring back at me, but I do not see my true self anymore. I see the person everybody tells me I am. My sisters like to call me pork chop and say I am fat, so do the kids at school. My Mom says I do not wash my hair and that it looks greasy. My Dad said that if I do not keep my hands and fingernails clean that everybody will think I am dirty and not like me. These are the people that love me and I know they are telling me all of this because it is true. I am a dirty, fat, greasy little girl that people are not going to like. I began to cry looking at myself in that mirror. What am I going to do now? I hate myself. I repeated this behavior most days throughout my childhood. I still today will stare in the mirror and think many of those same thoughts and more. You see as I went through life every time someone said something to me I held on to it good or bad. The bad of course were much more believable for me so the bad has tended to linger much longer than the good.

Our Mirrors started out clean without a streak on it. As we went through childhood and someone said or did something to us, we created a rule for ourselves. If you happened to hear, "You have fuzzy hair." That comment made you place a rule on your mirror and once on your mirror it stuck. Now as you look into your mirror you see yourself starring back with fuzzy hair. "You have a big nose", another rule you may have heard. You now see yourself with fuzzy hair and a big nose. I know it sounds silly but it is true. Take a moment and think about everything you do not like about yourself. Then think back the first time you heard someone else say it to you. Chances are it was someone else that pointed out something in you that they viewed as a flaw and told you, so you too now think it is a flaw. It is not a flaw. It is who you are. All these rules we place on a mirror makes it harder and harder for us to see our true self staring back at us. Now all we see is this disfigured image that we believe define us as a person. Well it doesn't.

The rules we place on our mirror are not all physical. We set rules for ourselves on everything. Some of my rules are, ghosts are not real to I talk too much. Whatever you are told and reinforced is your set of rules you live by. Every time you look at your life through your mirror your rules are always there for you to follow. Keep in mind that everyone's rules when it comes to their appearance to the way they act can be different. So when you do not understand why that person in front of you at the deli is throwing a fit over the fact that the deli man happened to grab the wrong imported ham; know that someone either showed or told them it was ok to speak out their feelings regardless of where they are or who may hear. Everybody is different. It is ok; you do not need to accept anybody but yourself. You do not need to clean anyone else's mirror except your own. As you start to erase your rules you will begin to understand where they came from and why the person in your life set those rules for you. Chances are someone set those rules for them and they are teaching you what they know, good or bad.

This mirror we have created for ourselves is a healthy thing. You see, our mirror, which house our rules also house our morale, our conscience, and what we view as acceptable behavior. Our mirror is who we are, how we feel, how we act and how we love. The mirror itself is not the problem. The problem is what is on our mirrors. When our mirrors are full of self deprecating things that is when it is a problem. The mirror houses all the bad things that have happened in our life that have a negative effect on our self esteem. You may have been abused throughout your child hood and when you confronted someone to help, you were told you were lying or told that you deserved it. You placed on your mirror, "I am a liar and I deserve the abuse." That is a lot on a child. When you are abused and start to believe there is nothing you can do and that you deserve the abuse it begins a cycle of self abuse. You will invite abuse into your life. You will be drawn to people who abuse you. The reason why is because that is what you know. That is what you are comfortable with and grow to expect in life. You may not think "I am going to date this person because he will hit me and yell at me and I love it." No, it is not that obvious. It is a self worth you have placed on yourself deep down inside. You want happiness and for everyone to treat you good. When they do treat you good it makes you feel a bit uncomfortable and untrusting. For me, when someone was kind to me all the time I would think "Why are they being so nice? What did they do? What do they want?" I never just took it as they were being nice because they cared for me and liked me for who I am. As I grew up and my mirror was covered with the idea of being fat, greasy, and dirty and that no one will like me, that is when my downward spiral of myself worth got lower and lower. I grew up in house with a mother that did the best she could with what she knew in life. However, my mother suffered from so many of her own problems that she did not take ownership of. She did not try to get help and because of her own personal problems they were reflected out into the way she treated her children. My mother was not any different than anyone else. You are what you are taught.

I am the youngest of four children, all girls, and during my childhood, my mother's favorite. I do not remember a lot about my childhood but I do remember my mom seemed to love me more. I use to lay with her in bed as she rubbed my head while we watched TV. When she was sad she always held on tight to me like she did not want to let go. I think I made her feel better. My sisters resented that my mom showed me more affection then them. They called me "The Favorite" and would wonder "why mom doesn't love me as much as Stacy", which sounds great for me, but the constant resentment from my sisters at such a young age caused me to place a rule on my mirror; "people think I am better than them." The fact that deep down I did not like myself very much and the idea that people think that I believe I am better, I did everything in my power to make people believe that I do not think I'm better. This has turned into me apologizing for everything I do. If I breathe and someone next to me happens to feel my breath, I apologize. If I talk and I think I talked to loud, I apologize. If I walk in a room and someone quickly looks up at me, I apologize. I must say I'm sorry at least 100 times a day. It all stems back to the fact my sisters were jealous that my mom paid more attention to me in their eyes.

Now that we have an understanding of what our mirror is, how it effects how we view ourselves and our actions let's start to recreate our mirror so we can have an understanding on where exactly to begin. I am sure as you were reading the words of this chapter things were coming to your mind about different times in your life someone said something to you that hurt, you believed them and wrote a rule on you mirror. Those experiences that pop into your mind first are what you need to start with. On a piece of paper or right in the border of this page write down everything you can think of that you do not like about yourself. This is how mine looks:

I am fat, I have greasy hair, I am dirty, talk too much, self-centered, people think I think I am better than them, smart, I deserve abuse, I hate myself, humor cures all, food always makes you feel better, never say no, trust no one, people are mean, life is not fair, I am ugly.

I could go on but we do not want 10 pages of this. You can have ten pages if you want, have as many as you need. If you only have one thing, it is ok. Then that one thing is where you need to start. If you are having trouble right now identifying your rules, do not worry. The next step, Life Map, we will be going over how to discover the rules you live your life by. There are many rules that are on our mirrors that consciously we have no idea that they are even there. The mirror is just the first step but as you will see all the steps merge together.

If you notice I wrote down smart as a negative. That is because I have always been told, "Oh you think you are so smart." Like being smart was a bad thing. Yes I am smart and proud to be smart. Some people I have met have been called beautiful their whole life and actually view it as a negative. They would hear people say to them, "I hate her because she is so pretty". Now, when a child hears that over and over again throughout their life they begin to resent the fact they are beautiful. As they grow up when someone calls them beautiful it actually makes them uncomfortable. They begin to believe that if they were not so beautiful maybe people would like them more. You see it is the little things that people say that they did not mean or they were only kidding that truly can hurt person. A lot of those things we hear once it may hurt our feelings but eventually we get over it. The things we hear day in and day out is what sticks. My sister is always saying to her daughter "Get off your big butt and come here." She is always kidding, she is even laughing the times she has said it. However, the fact that she says it more days then not has had a negative effect on her daughter. My sister's daughter is eleven years old and makes sure every shirt she wears covers her butt because she thinks she has a big butt. If you ask her, "Why do you think you have a big butt?" she just says, "Because I do." gets embarrassed and walks away pulling down her shirt. I know this type of thing sound harmless but it is not.

When completing your Mirror you have got to understand that the rules you live by were set mostly by your family and friends when you were a child. I have had some family members I have worked through this process with. When I begin the mirror process and start to talk about things that happened in my childhood they get instantly defensive. I have heard so many times from my family, "Oh I was only kidding, you need to get over it" or "Oh you think your life was so bad." What you need to understand about your mirror is it does not matter how other people view the experiences you have gone through. Everything that was either shown or told to you that you decided to keep as a rule for yourself is for a reason. How you interpreted the experiences is based upon what rules you needed to create for yourself. You created these rules for yourself because as you grew up you needed to make certain decisions. Those decisions you made got you into other situations that have contributed to your soul learning important life lessons. The problem being is for most people I have met they never stop allowing themselves to be a victim of their own life. Being a victim of your own life will ensure that you do not learn your lessons. If you do not learn your life lessons then you will continue to experience negative situations without understanding why. Understanding that each of us as individuals will take out of an experience what we need to for our life. This helps us understand why you can have two siblings raised exactly the same way but have a totally different view on life. Many times those two same siblings if questioned about their childhoods you will get two totally conflicting stories.

You did it! You started your journey of discovering all the negative rules on your mirror. You have taken your first step in becoming a leader of your own life. As we go through our life from the moment we are born to today, we have experiences whether good or bad that mold us into the person we are. The person you are is perfect. The person you are, is exactly who you are suppose to be and that is a good thing. Experiences in our lives that have yielded negative effects on our self-image have caused a war within us. You must know that there is no victor of war fought within. We now move on to understanding why certain things happen to us and how our rules on our mirrors have guided us to those situations.

Step Two: Life Map

When I was child my father injured his back severely. He was unable to work so my mother needed to find a job and financially support our entire family. My father stayed home to take care of us girls. My father was a father that was fun, he lived to laugh. He loved to prance around the house singing. He sang about everything. If he was cooking eggs he would make up a silly song about cooking eggs. This is something that I loved about my childhood. There was a lot of laughter when it came to my father and a lot of playing around. I find myself being the same way with my children today. With my father's easy going personality it was nice to have him around as a child. My mother, who was now working very hard to support a family, really had a hard time seeing the humor in my father's actions. When she would get home from work she was always very angry and resentful to my father. My father, being the joker that he is, would try to lighten the situation of my mother yelling at him with a joke. This just fueled my Mother's fire. My mother stopped thinking my father was funny and easy going and started to view him as lazy and useless. When this occurred it truly changed my childhood. As a child watching my mother and father fight constantly made me feel very uncomfortable around yelling. Til this day, if someone yells at me I get very upset. Watching my parents' behavior set rules for me on how I handle confrontation. When I have a disagreement with someone I keep it to myself and push it down into my gut and do not speak about it. I believe that if I confronted that person about my disappointment then a fight would start. Instead I just keep everything to myself because I cannot stand yelling and I cannot stand the idea that someone might be mad at me.

My father, who would try to lighten every situation with a joke, created a rule on my mirror as well. Humor will make it all better. Humor really does not make it all better. Now every time I am confronted with a situation that makes me feel uncomfortable I laugh. I laugh at myself constantly and make jokes about myself. For example I always refer to myself as a big girl. I make jokes about myself being overweight to everyone especially those that I just met. The reason why is because I want to make sure they know I know I am overweight so there is no need to bring it up. I would rather point out my own flaws and make a joke about it. I wanted everyone to know that I already knew what my flaws were. So, there is no reason for them to point out my flaws. I also tell everyone I talk too much because if they say it to me it hurts a lot worse than if I say it. This really is not a good thing. This behavior has caused many people to give me weird looks. Then of course once they have a weird look I will crack another joke about making fun of myself. So, I again will feel better and they will not point out that I am weird about making fun of myself. It all sounds a bit ridiculous and confusing but I have mastered this unhealthy technique. All of this stems back to my father showing me that humor cures all and my mother showing me that confrontation is always bad. You see I have a bridge that connects me to experiences in my childhood that I do not want to relive. I do everything that I can to try to avoid people making fun of me by me making fun of myself. I avoid confrontation when someone is upset with me by laughing or making a joke. I always point out what I think are my flaws so no one will make fun of me. I do everything I can so I do not have to get upset and I do not have to have any type of confrontation with them regarding anything they may have possible said to me. Wow, it seems even crazier when I write it all down. But this is how my mind works. So what do I do to fix it?

We must take our next step to turn our life of a victim to a life of a leader. In the previous chapter we recreated our mirror of rules we live our life by and uncovered those rules that we set for ourselves that created a negative self image. During this next step we are going to look at our rule, figure out why we put it on our mirror and how it affects our lives today.

As we live our life every day we go through different experiences that define us as a person. Those experiences we undergo are there in order to help us learn an important life lesson. You see, before we were born we lived in Heaven with God. In Heaven life is perfect, it is divine. In order for our souls to evolve and become closer to God we must learn important lessons. Those important lessons we are not able to learn while we live in Heaven due to the fact that in order for us to learn something we must be tested. A test is the only way we can truly understand if we learned something. Being that heaven is perfect those tests cannot be performed there. Therefore God created Earth. Earth for us is our souls' school. Earth is designed to experience the negative and test us.

The first thing we must do is like when we recreated our mirrors, we need to recreate and uncover the life lesson our souls have already been trying to learn. Before we were born we created our life's outline of what we wanted our souls to undergo in order to learn the lessons we felt were important to this life. We mapped out our life prior to being born. Knowing that we are human and that we do not typically learn our lesson the first time we experience something, we have built into our life map many experiences to ensure we do learn what we need to. Our life maps are extremely intricate. They start with your parents. Yes, you chose who you wanted as parents and siblings if any. The reason we picked our parents is because we wrote into our life map that they would be certain type of people who will set the foundation of who we will be in life. You knew coming here that they would treat you a certain way and set certain rules for you. They would be the first people to start to create your mirror. This information may be a bit far-fetched for some people to understand or even believe so I want to show you. Let's begin by recreating your life map. This process may take some time to complete. I want to give you the information you need to start. You can continue to uncover you life Map for as long as you may need to do it. Start by thinking about your mirror and some rules that may be on it. For me I want to start with, "I deserve abuse."

As I grew up in a house that was full of fighting, making fun of each other and saying things to hurt each other's feelings, I came to think this type of behavior was just the way life was. Feeling bad about yourself was normal. Being abused mentally was normal and because of this I found myself at the age of 15 in a relationship that made my childhood seem easy. As I spoke about in chapter one when you are abused as a child you begin to accept the abuse and believe you deserve the abuse. Once this happens you put a self worth on yourself that is very low. This type of behavior is what invites abusers into your life. For me it was my first long term boyfriend named Steve. I met Steve through a mutual friend I had gone to school with. Steve was three years older than me, which does not seem like a large age difference now but when a 15 year old is dating an 18 year old they are truly worlds apart. Steve was a very angry person and verbally abusive. He tried to control everything I did. I could not dress a certain way, I could not go certain places, and I could not talk to any other boy except for him and his friends, but only if he was around. Steve did not put on an act at all. These behaviors started right when we began to hang out. In my mind this type of behavior was normal. I believed that because he loved me so much he cared about what I did and did not want me to get hurt. He was just very protective. Steve used fear to control me and to have me do whatever he wanted me to do. One afternoon he picked me up from school and we went to a fast food restaurant to eat. He ordered all the food and as the cashier was placing it on our tray, a boy I went to school with hollered over to me, "Hello Stacy how are you?" That was all that was said. I gave a quick wave and put my hand down fast knowing as soon as I did that Steve was not going to be happy. Steve whipped his face over at me, gave me a look of death and I knew I was in trouble. He grabbed the tray of food and walked over to where he wanted to sit. I followed him with my head down - I was scared to look at him. He was still sowling and went to sit down, but did not get all the way into his chair. He took the tray of food and threw it at me. Soda and all went everywhere and he began to scream. I could not even tell you what he was saying. I tried to pick up the food but he was already dragging me out of there yelling. He was upset that a boy from school said hello. A woman ran out behind us screaming at him to stop. He lunged at her and she ran back inside. We got in his truck and began to drive. At this point I began to cry. I told him I wanted to go home. He just continued to yell. He grabbed my purse and my wallet and threw all of my stuff out of the window while we were driving. He dropped me off at my house and I ran out of the truck and into my front door. For 15 minutes he drove in front of my house back and forth burning the rubber of his tires. Then he left. He came and picked me up from the school the very next day and we continued on our relationship liked nothing happened. This type of behavior was very common and to be honest not too much different then what I was use to. However Steve took it to another level. He yelled at me and abused me regardless of where he was or who was with us. He did not care. I continued my relationship with Steve for almost 9 years until the age of 24. In that time the abuse got greater and greater and turned very physical. What made me eventually leave Steve was he stepped over the line. What I mean by that is when you do not have very high self worth and abuse yourself it is amazing how much abuse you can take from other people. No matter how mean someone is to you they could never be meaner than you are to yourself and that is your line. Your line is the level at which you abuse yourself. What crossed me over the line was not the physical or mental abuse I underwent for so many years, it was when his mother said something to me and that was it, I was done. Steve treated me the same way his father treated his mother. Steve was taught that you must dominate and conquer your woman. That Men were the boss and what they wanted they got. Steve's Mom went through this type of life for 20 plus years. Steve's parents had nothing in life. They did not have a home, they were living with us. They did not have a car, they were driving mine. Steve's mom weighed probably 250 or so pounds and was miserable. She walked up to me one Saturday night looked me straight in the face and said, "Do you want to end up just like me?" I said, "No." and she said, "Well you are going to." She was right I was going to. She was my line. I knew then I did not deserve to have to live a life like hers. I left the next morning and never went back. Though I did not learn the lesson I needed to learn about abuse. I did not learn that I do not deserve abuse. I only learned that I had a line of how much abuse I can take.

When developing your life Map it is best to write it out. You can use the border of this book or the note pages in the back. As you are reading write down notes on certain experiences you have gone through in your life. It is best done on a separate piece of paper. I have chosen - I do not deserve abuse- to work on first because for me it really covers a lot of rules that I placed on my mirror. Throughout my child hood the constant name calling, pointing out of my physical flaws as well as all the yelling and hateful things that occurred in my life all to me fit into "I deserve abuse." My first step is to understand I do not deserve to be abused by anyone and I do not have the right to abuse anyone else. Before I knew that "I do not deserve abuse" was one of my life lessons I needed to learn, I had to write out my life Map. During this activity you will fill out all of the experiences you have gone through in life. As you do that you will see a common thread that links them together. How you begin writing out your life map is by creating a chart. While you are creating your chart think about the rules you have placed on your mirror. You will see a connection or I like to call a bridge that links how you ended up in a certain situation and how you handled that situation due to rules on your mirror. Let's begin by outlining your chart then you can work on filling it in. As you are creating your chart, which will turn into your Life Map, you do not need to write a full explanation as to what occurred if you do not want to. Be brief you know what happened, or write out as much as you need to. Here is an example of a blank life map.

Age	Experience - Personal Relationships	Experience - Friendships	Experience - Work	Experience - Your Self	Rules	People

You will want to begin by filling in each part of the chart. You can begin with whatever situation that comes to mind first. The chart is divided into 7 columns. Here are the descriptions of each column:

Age: The approximate age you were when the situation occurred.

Experience – Personal Relationships: Complete if the situation had to do with your personal relationships. Personal relationships include family members, Spouses, Boyfriends and Girlfriends.

Experience – Friendships: Complete if the situation had to do with Friends or acquaintances.

Experience – Work: Complete if the situation had to with your career.

Experience – Yourself: Complete if the situation is about things you have done or are doing to yourself.

Rules: What rules on your mirror contributed to getting into this situation? What rules on your mirror were created because of this situation?

Person: What person or people did this situation involve?

Here is how my Life Chart looked when I began this process.

Age	Experience - Personal Relationships	Experience - Friendships	Experience - Work	Experience - Your Self	Rules	People
8				viewed my physical appearance negatively started overeating and sneaking food for comfort	I am fat I'm ugly I'm Dirty Greasy Hair	Mother Father Sisters Kids at School
15	Started Dating Steve	Pushed away friends in my life because of Steve		Started smoking regularly	I deserve abuse	Myself and Steve

This is a small version of a life Map but it gives you the idea on how to complete it. In the workbook section of this book I we go over again how to complete your Life Map. You want to fill it in using any experiences you feel are relevant. What column you start with depends on what you are trying to figure out. If you have a rule you know you live your life by and you want to figure out why. Begin by writing that rule in the rule column. Then ask yourself, "When was the last time this rule affected my life?" Write about that situation. Then think about the next time and so on. What this activity does is it will trigger your memories on experiences that contributed to that rule. Eventually you will narrow it down far enough to convince yourself that you obviously need to change that rule. Do not second guess yourself. If you are thinking about it then write it. I have worked with many people who out of conversation I have discovered that it is the little things that matter. If it pops into your mind, even if you do not know why, write it down. You can also fill out your Life Map starting with one topic such as work experiences and then move onto the next. Fill it out how ever you want. Most importantly be honest with yourself. We have been given a set of rules to live by with our mirrors and on those mirrors many of us have learned some negative things that we show through our own actions. Growing up I too made fun of people and I too yelled and acted in ways I am not proud of. Most people have. Why I am saying this is because if you want to truly help yourself learn your lesson so you can let it go you must be true to yourself through the entire process.

As you are completing your life map you will see a pattern of certain things pop up. For me it was the abuse. I went from my childhood to dating Steve to then moving right into another relationship with a man named Paul. Paul definitely had some issues and he too was very verbally abusive. Though not as aggressively as Steve. Paul always made me feel like I thought I was better and made me feel bad about it. I felt like I had to apologize for who I was as a person. Paul made me feel like I was mean to him and did not show him I cared about him. Whenever I would talk to him he would tell me to shut up that he had heard it before and that all I do is talk. Comparing Paul to Steve, I never really thought at the time that Paul was abusive. While writing out my map I saw a definite connection. After dating Paul I began dating Scott, who is now my husband. Scott does not abuse me in any way shape or form.

He is kind, loving and accepting to me in every way. However, at the same time I began to date Scott I started a new position with a financial firm in Portsmouth, NH. My boss at the time was very abusive to me. He discriminated against women and did so very openly. He would say many things to me that were hateful and tried to ruin my career. I ended up leaving that job fairly quickly because I noticed my pattern while completing my Life Map. I invited people who abuse me into my life. As I was writing my map I discovered all the situations that I experienced all showed signs right away of abuse. I just did not pay attention because I was blurred by my own inequalities through the rules on my mirror. If it was not for sitting down and really going over all the situations in my life I would never have realized I do not deserve abuse. So now, if a person comes into my life and they begin to treat me in a certain way, or I see them treating other people in a certain way, I know what type of person they are right away. I do not allow myself to get into any type of abusive situations. You see by learning my lesson I now know if an abusive situation is rising and I know not to get involved. By making these connections to all the situations you have been through in life and seeing the bridge that brings you back to your mirror of rules, will make it possible for you to learn your lesson and not find yourself in the same situation again.

For me it has been hard to bring up so much of my past through the writing of my Life Map. Things happened in my life that I never really thought were significant. By going through the exercise of writing it all down I noticed so many things that could have and should have had a different outcome. They didn't due to my own issues that are buried deep down inside me. My father taught me that humor is suppose to cure all and he also told me that food will always make you feel better and to this day I use food to shelter myself from everything. If I am sad and I eat something I feel better. If I am bored and I eat something I feel better. If I am angry and I sink my teeth into a chocolate cookie it seems with every bite I take the frustration seems to melt away. It really is crazy. As I completed my Map I saw so much of it that bridged back to my mirror and my one big rule of not liking my physical appearance seemed to dominate and that makes me feel so sad and helpless. Due to that reality of my physical appearance making me feel so bad I turn to the one thing that causes so much of my physical appearance to be what I do not want it to be, and that is food.

I could go on and on about all the revelations I had while completing my life map. So many situations whether good or bad that made so much sense to me. When you are completing your life map make sure you include everything. You may start with the big experiences but do not forget the small experiences either. Our lives are like a giant puzzle. If we miss just once piece you can still tell what the picture is suppose to be but it will never be quite right.

Step Three: Intentions

We have learned about our mirror and learned how to complete our Life Map. We have all realized that the experiences we undergo throughout our lives create rules that we live our life by. These rules help guide us into situations that occur in order for us to learn life lessons. If we do not learn the life lesson we want our souls to learn we find ourselves right back in the same type of situation again and again. That is why you have heard so many people say "Why does this always happen to me?" That is because there is something they are suppose to learn from those experiences and the longer it takes them to learn it the longer they will be in that situation or another situation just like it.

As you create your Life Map and see your bridge that brings you back to your mirror, you are helping your soul learn your lessons. Finding out that there is a lesson you have been trying to learn and realizing you are being tested over and over again throughout your life is an amazing thing. It is a breakthrough. However, just because we see there is a connection and a life lesson to be learned, is not the end for us. We still have the mirror of rules we live by. We still have been mentally damaged by certain experiences we have had. We understand why we see ourselves a certain way because we understand our mirrors now. We understand that everyone acts differently based upon what rules we learned throughout our lives that we placed on our mirrors. We understand that certain situations arise in our lives in order for us to learn our life lessons, we all understand that. The next step in turning your life of a victim to a life of a leader is through intention. This is the hardest step. This is the step that will change the way you view yourself and other people. This is the step that may take years to master but every day that you work on this step you will see a definite change within you and your life for the better.

My mind is the biggest problem. Even as I sit here trying to write the words of this chapter I am psyching myself out by thinking I cannot explain exactly what an intention is. That thought of "I can't" is what's making me sit, type and erase for the last half an hour or so now. My thought of not being able to do something is an intention I have set; an intention that is making it impossible for me to do something I want to do. We all do this to ourselves every day over everything. Ultimately an intention is your desired outcome. You want to ensure that your intentions are always positive.

With all the experiences we have had as children and young adults that have molded us in the person we are today we choose different means to cope with that stress. Some of us push it down into our gut and never speak of it and deny it. Some of us cast blame on other people like our parents, siblings, friends and other people that may have been involved with the abuse. Some of us act out in aggressive manners such as yelling and fighting with the ones we hold dearest. Some of us seek out other means to suppress the pain with drugs and alcohol. We all do what we feel we need to do in order to mask the reality of what happened to us throughout our lives. We all have different levels of abuse from name calling, physical abuse, sexual abuse or people in our lives denied us love. There are so many unhealthy actions that we have all experienced. No matter how intense the abuse is, it is all relevant and all just as important as someone else's abuse.

I have worked with people that have sexual issues. Some of those issues were due to childhood sexual abuse. Some were due to not experiencing affection from a parent. There have been many different reasons as to why people have issue when it comes to intimacy. For me the problem with intimacy surfaced after I married my husband and began our family. This took a long time for me to truly uncover the mystery of "why do I feel sick when I am intimate with my husband?" It was not the closeness we have. It was not the intimacy of showing our love for each other. It was not the touching and holding, it was the actual act of sex itself. The first couple of years of our marriage, I kept this to myself. I knew it was an issue. I kept putting it to the back burner while I was creating my Life Map. It was like I did not even want to deal with it. However by not dealing with it, so I could let it go, I created an intention that the problem is here, I know it and there is nothing I can do about it. By creating that intention of "I have a problem and I can't do anything about it.", that is exactly what happened. I could not do anything about it, except watch and feel as my problem became larger; to the point I would be ill at the thought of having sex with my husband. I would try to avoid it as much as possible; which, was not that often considering he wanted it every day. Knowing that I love him more than anything in the world, I would just suffer through it and not tell him a thing. Was that really fair to him? No of course not. Instead of keeping it down inside my gut I verbalized it. I admitted it and took ownership of my problem. By doing that I set the intention that I wanted it to stop and I wanted it to go away. Now, that I have set the intention that

I wanted this problem to go away; I first needed to understand when the issue began in my life. How you uncover what situations in your life created a rule on your mirror, mine being that "I am uncomfortable with sex", is through your Life Map. I decided to start a new column and named it "sex". I then started brainstorming every sexual partner I have had and anytime that something happened to me that was negative in regards to sex. What I narrowed down to and saw was a common thread; that sex always had to do with my partner making something up to me. Most of my experiences were with Steve, since I was with him for so long. Every time he would abuse me mentally and physically he would try to apologize with sex. In his mind, he thought, by having sex with me, he was showing affection and that he loved me. He felt that the sex would make up for the hitting, choking and name calling. I learned to associate sex with disgust. Disgust is what I felt towards him and myself for allowing him to be intimate with me after the way he acted. I allowed him to be intimate because I was so afraid of him, which made me feel out of control and unsafe. Being afraid and unsafe, relates me back to an experience when I was 15 years old. I was raped by a boy I went to school with. It was like I was reliving those emotions I had during the rape. Steve did not rape me, but he made me feel helpless and dirty, just like I did the day I was raped. My first experience of sex was by being raped. My first experience with consensual sex was with an abuser. I wrote the rule on my mirror that "sex made me feel uncomfortable, out of control and unsafe". This rule followed me into my marriage.

Now that I have made the connection, I am able to let it go. To ensure that I truly let go of the emotion that were caused by my negative experiences I do that through intention. I set the intention of "I can change my rule on my mirror". I can let it go and never bring it back.

To begin the process of setting positive intentions in your life you must first create a new positive mirror of rules. In chapter one we talked about what negative rules are on your mirror. Some of my negative rules were:

I am fat, I have greasy hair, I am dirty, talk too much, self centered, people think I think I am better than them, smart, I deserve abuse, I hate myself, humor cures all, food always makes you feel better, never say no, trust no one, people are mean, life is not fair, I am ugly, sex makes me sick.

Now that you know some of your negative rules, you can begin to recreate new positive rules to live your life by. How you create new rules in your life is by writing down all of the negative rules that were placed on your mirror. Next to each negative rule, write something positive about yourself. Here is how mine looks:

I am fat – I am beautiful

I have Greasy Hair - Blonde Beautiful Curls

I am Dirty – Clean

Talk too much – I love a good conversation

Self Centered – I care about people

People think I think I am better than them – My life is great and I deserve it

Smart – Smart

I deserve abuse – No one abuses me

I hate myself – I love myself

Humor cures all – I am not a joke

Food always makes you feel better – I make myself feel better

Never say No – I do what is best for me

Trust no one – trust those that can be trusted

People are mean – Everyone has their own Life Map

Life is not fair – Life is what you make it

I am ugly – I am pretty

Sex makes me sick – I am safe

Once you have completed turning your negative rules into your new positive rules, you will need to remind yourself of these new rules every day. Your negative rules were continuously reinforced to you throughout your life. It is now your turn to change those rules. Your new positive rules must also be reinforced every day. Since of course we are all no longer small children, we have to reinforce them to ourselves. How we do that is by creating a picture of those rules and placing them by a mirror in our home. Every day you need to read those rules to yourself and believe them. By reading aloud your new rules you are setting an intention for yourself each and every day.

Here is what mine looks like:

I am not a joke   Smart   *Blonde beautiful curls*

My life is great, I deserve it

Trust those that can be trusted   *I do what is best for me*

Clean   Life is what you make it

I make myself feel better   *I love a good conversation*

No one abuses me

I am safe

Everyone has their own Life Map

I am beautiful

I LOVE myself

I care about people

These positive rules begin the process of setting positive intentions in your life and beginning to replace the negative rules on your mirror.

While you continue the process of writing out your Life Map you will continue to uncover all the negative rules that you have placed on your mirror. You have to change that negative rule into something positive, believe it and begin to live your life with that new positive rule. Once you discover a negative rule you are living your life by, you must turn that rule into a new positive rule and add it to your positive mirror. The act of writing down the new rule is great. However, you have to reinforce it day in and day out. That is why I had you physically write things down and put it in a place where you are able to see it every day and read it every day.

All of your challenging experiences, throughout your life, have been a constant reminder of your negative rules. You started to believe these rules and follow these rules. It is now your turn, to set positive rules and have positive reinforcement in your life. The more you see it, the more you hear it, the more you will truly believe the positive. Intentions lead your life. Your intention is what is deep down inside your soul. Your true feelings you hide within yourself, about yourself, which you may never verbalize to anyone else. These are the rules we need to change. The only way to do that is to set the intention of "I can" and believe it and recite it to yourself every day.

Step Four: Forgiveness

Intentions are strong and it is very challenging to change your intentions that are deep down within yourself, without addressing forgiveness as well at the same time.

Forgiveness is something many of us have not truly given to many people. The reason why is because those people are our excuses; our anchor to our mental issues we all face. We all feel as though we have to blame someone including ourselves. We must stop. Stop with the excuses. Stop with the poor me. Stop living your life as a victim.

First, let's all set the intention of "I will forgive". The most effective way of truly forgiving someone, is by having the understanding and acceptance that every single person is living a life that is fulfilling their own lessons. Every person has gone through experiences in their life that have defined them into the person they are. Every person has a Mirror and a Life Map. Believe that because it is true. For me the biggest person I had to forgive was Steve. Once I truly understood my own Mirror and my own Life Map, forgiving Steve was quite simple.

I began my process of forgiving Steve by thinking about his Life Map. Having an understanding of what a mean and hateful person he was, I began to think of all the mean and hateful things he must have gone through. Those negative experiences he went through created rules on his mirror that defined who he is in life. Steve too had many self deprecating things on his mirror. He treated me the only way he knew how, which was the way he was taught. Once I began to recreate Steve's Mirror and Life Map; based upon who he was as a person and what information I knew about his life, Steve's actions began to make sense to me. Once I understood Steve, in this new way, I actually began to feel sorry for him. I turned my hatred for him, my resentfulness and my anger into pity. Once I was able to do that forgiveness naturally followed.

Steve acted the only way he knew how. He was taught how to act, how to love and how to hate from his own experiences through his life. Those experiences created rules he lived by. Just like me, Steve had his own Mirror, his own Life Map and his own lessons to learn. Steve helped me learn lessons as well, and for that I thank him. He did for me in my life exactly what I needed him to do.

For each person that you are holding onto as an excuse, as to why you are the way you are, you must do the same with them, as I did with Steve. You must forgive them. How you figure out what people you need to forgive is through the process of your Life Map. The people that influenced your life and reinforced or created a rule on your mirror are the ones you must forgive. You must understand how and why they did what they did, as you are writing down each experience. Each person who has taught you how to be who you are is living out their own Life Map; which is influenced by their mirror in order to learn their own life lessons. They did to you, exactly what they were suppose to do. Understand that and believe it, so you are able to make sense of it and let it go.

Most people I talk to have issue with their parents. I talked briefly about my mother in the first two chapters. I spoke about my mother doing things that some people may view as abusive. Some people, including my sisters, may say my mother was abusive to her children and husband. I say my mother did exactly what I needed her to do, for me. My mother raised me, and I have become a remarkable woman and an amazing mother. What she taught me was not all bad. My mother is a person that has had a huge impression in my life, more than she will ever know. My mother has lived a life just like everyone else, that made her in to the person she is today. By her being who she is and treating me the way she did, has made it possible for me to get myself into situations. Those situations enabled me to learn my life lessons, so I can evolve my soul to be closer to God. Without my mother none of this would have been possible. So to my mother, thank you.

Intentions and forgiveness go hand and hand. You must always ensure you have positive intentions. How you do that is by reinforcing what your intentions is. Every morning when you wake up, say out loud, "It is going to be a good day! It is going to be a good day! It is going to be a good day!" Make yourself believe it. Whatever your desired outcome is is your intention. Ensure that your desires are positive in everything you do.

Let's take some time to add some new positive rules and intentions to your mirror. I want everyone to write "I am living a life of a leader". Every day when you recite your positive mirror to yourself, I want you to say, "I am living a life of a leader". Whenever you are faced with a trying situation in your life I want you to ask yourself, "Would someone that is a leader of their own life, make this decision this way?" Really think about it for a moment. At first you will find yourself answering no. The more you do this the more your instinct of doing the right thing for you, will take over. You will begin to answer your own question with a yes. Now is the time to really analyze yourself. I want you to think before you act. Think about what you say before you let it out of your mouth. If what you are about to say has the word "I can't" do not say it. Change it to "I can." If the words that are about to come out of your mouth are in any way going to reflect you or anyone else in a negative way, rethink your choice of words. In order to change your intentions to positive, you must first not allow yourself to continually be brought down by a negative mind set. You may still be thinking negatively inside your head. The more you make yourself speak and act in a positive manner, the more your frame of mind will change.

On your new positive mirror, write down anything you want to change in your life. Write down your goals. Your mirror is very effective in reminding you of what you truly are and what you are capable of. Whatever you write on it, make it positive and make sure you constantly remind yourself of it every day. Many people I have worked with also write their goals, of what they are working on, on small pieces of paper and keep it with them for a constant reminder. Eventually they stop reading the note and just believe it. You will too.

Step Five: Spirit Guides

We have completed our journey of what we need to do to turn our life of a victim to a life a leader. I now want to begin to speak about the tools that God has given us, to help us, through our life journey. These are tools you have been using already throughout your life, although you may not have realized exactly how to use the tools or what their intended purpose is for. These tools are used to better your life, to understand your purpose, to understand your life goals and to succeed by learning your lessons so you may evolve your soul and become closer to God.

Spirit Guides have been given to us here in this life to help guide us in the right direction, in our life journey. Although we may never hear or see our guides, it does not mean they are not right there with us every step of the way. When we left the comfort of the other side to begin our life of bettering our souls, to become closer to God, we were given tools to assist us. I believe the most important tool is your Spirit Guide.

Spirit Guides are your direct connection to the Divine. Your Spirit Guides are a personal guide that you have had by your side since the moment you were born into this world. They walk next to you in spirit, constantly. Before you were born you wrote out your Life Map and decided what experiences you will undergo to learn the lessons you chose to learn in this life. Your Spirit Guide is the one that was right there next to you through that entire process. You and your guide created an agreement before you came to earth to live your life. That agreement was for them to be by your side through all of it. They will give you gentle nudges in the right direction, when you are heading down a difficult path. They are your inner voice that tells you when something is just not right. They are the one that you can rely on regardless of what is happening in your life. Spirit guides are a true gift that God has given us.

Spirit guides are here to help point you in the right direction when faced with a difficult decision. Have you ever done something and got a feeling in your stomach that made you feel like maybe, "I should not do this"? Or a feeling of, "I just know I am suppose to do this"? That feeling is your Spirit Guide helping you along.

A few facts about your guide:

- They will not interfere with your decision making. They will only help you, by guiding you in the right direction. You have the ultimate choice of what you decide to do, better known as free will.

- They are spirits that live on the other side. They have never lived with you in this world. Although you probably have spirits of past over loved ones all around you and guiding you as well, they are not your Spirit Guides

- You chose your Spirit Guide before you left the other side to live your life here.

- Spirit Guides, a lot of times, have also lived here on earth as well just at an earlier time. They do understand the struggles you face every day.

- Some people have more than one spirit guide.

Spirit Guides are given to us as a tool from God. Keep that in mind. Spirit Guides are always there for your best interest. They will never mean any ill will to you or another person. Spirit Guides will never create havoc in your life. They will only guide you throughout your life path; assisting you with guidance and Love.

Your Spirit Guide has been with you through your entire life. Anxiously awaiting some type of acknowledgement of their existence by you, this, is a compliment to them. When I first learned about my Spirit Guide I found it helpful to set a sign for them. Your sign, you choose, will be your confirmation that your Spirit Guide is with you. Select a sign and you will see it pop up everywhere. My sign for my Spirit Guide is Lady Bugs. As soon as I set my sign I saw lady bugs everywhere. Even in the middle of winter. You set the sign to start convincing yourself of their existences. Some people just believe they are there. Others need a bit of convincing. Your sign can be absolutely anything from butterflies to deer. It does not matter. Also I began to thank my Spirit Guides every night before I went to bed. I still do this every night. The reason being is I know I am a lot of work and I am grateful for their assistance. Start tonight by thanking your guides. They love to be acknowledged in anyway.

You do have the ability to be able to meet your Spirit Guide. I find the best way to do that is through a guided meditation. I have written a very effective meditation that when done correctly every person I have done this guided meditation for has been able to start a line of communication with their Spirit Guide. When you first do it you may only get a piece of information such as your Spirit Guide's name, if they are a man or women, what color hair, etc. Once you recognize your Spirit Guide and truly believe they are there with you every day, the better you will feel. You will know that you are never alone no matter what you do in this life.

The best way to do this guided meditation is to create a relaxing environment. Have another person read aloud the following guided meditation or record the meditation and play it back to yourself. The first time you do it, it will be best if you hear exactly what you are supposed to envision, after you will be able to revisit it again on your own. You can also visit www.ahigherenergy.net and click on the Spirit Guide Tab. I have recorded this same meditation on the site.

Before you begin your meditation have a pen and paper ready, to journal all that you saw, felt, heard or just knew. Describe your Spirit Guide. Did they tell you their name? Are they a man or women? What did they look like, feel like or sound like? Whatever information you received write it down.

Spirit Guide Meditation

Take a deep breath through your nose and hold it 1....2....3.... and let it out through your mouth. Let all of the air in your lungs out hold it 1....2....3.......

Take a deep breath through your nose and hold it 1....2....3.... and let it out through your mouth. Let all of the air in your lungs out hold it 1....2....3.......

Take a deep breath through your nose and hold it 1....2....3.... and let it out through your mouth. Let all of the air in your lungs out hold it 1....2....3.......

Begin to breathe normally with your eyes closed every time you hear your breath coming in to your lungs and then out you become more and more relaxed.

In and out.......in and out........in and out.........

You are standing in the middle of a dirt road and you begin to walk down the road you see on your right side a path that leads through a small field. Take that path...

As you are walking through the small field you notice the path turns slightly to the left..........

Continue walking on the path..................

The sun is bright but the weather is cool. You hear so many wonderful noises. You here a hawk and look up to him in flight over the field........

As you continue on your path you notice that the path leads into the woods..........

Continue on your path..........

As you are walking down the path through the woods you look up and admire the beauty of the leaves they are starting to turn to so many shades of orange.........yellow..........red............

You take a deep breath you can smell autumn in the air a small breeze blows and it gives a bit of goose bumps on your arms.

Listen to the noises of nature.......... birds chirping.......... Ruffling of leaves...........scratching of branches...............

You see a small chipmunk run across the path just up in front of you..............

Continue down the path............

You start to notice you are beginning to descend......

You are now walking down a hill......

The hill is very easy to walk down. You feel very safe and know that you will not fall.....

The closer you get to the bottom of the hill the trees start to thin.......

You begin to notice sand beneath your feet......

You can hear waves.........

As you come to the bottom of the hill you emerge on to a beach.........

Walk along the beach......................

It is a beautiful day..........

As you are walking down the beach you see there is a small hut right up in front of you........

Go to the hut.........

The hut is empty.....

Sit down on the sand in the middle of the hut and close your eyes...........

You can hear yourself breathe and you feel the rays of sun coming through the holes in the roof.

Keep your eyes closed.........breathing in and out

You feel someone enter the hut with you keep your eyes closed.......

You feel them sit down in front of you.......

Reach out your hand and allow them to take it........

Open your eyes.........This is your Spirit Guide.....

Is your guide a man or women......what do they look like....... Take some time with your guide talk with them......

Walk with them back up the hill and allow them to guide you back while you talk. Take as much time as you need.

Now you have created a sacred place for you and your guide. You can visit this beach side hut whenever you would like to communicate directly with your Spirit Guides. You must know your Spirit Guides are with you always. I choose to speak with my Spirit Guide, inside my head, when I am trying to figure something out or if I am worried about something. I lean to my spirit guide for everything. They know all my deepest feelings and they help me figure things out. Your Spirit Guides are there to assist you in your life, not give you all the answers all the time. Remember our Spirit Guides will help as much as they can. They will lead us in the right direction and keep us out of trouble, but you have free will to make your own decisions. Keep in mind you need to listen, accept and act on their advice. They do not just make things happen for you.

Step Six: Dream Interpretation, Meditation and Signs

Dream Interpretation

Dreams really are amazing - they are messages from the beyond to help you figure out issues in your life. They are trying to decode the worries you have within your mind caused from your struggles in ever day life. Some people dream in the form of nightmares, others dream as if it is regular life. Whichever way you dream know they are full of answers you have been seeking. I recommend that you start a dream journal. Although we do dream every night, we do not always remember the dream. If we do, we usually remember most of it when we wake, but as the day goes on the visions of your dream fade until you only remember a little bit and sometimes none of the dream at all. You must keep a notebook with a pen on your nightstand so as soon as you wake, you can start writing every detail you can remember even if it makes no sense. Continue this daily. Do realize some mornings you wake you may not remember or think you did not have a dream the previous night. Know you did dream it just was not necessary for you to remember that information. It's ok not to remember as long as you always journal those dreams you do remember. As time goes on and you revisit your dream journal you will be amazed that answers you have been seeking were given to you.

It's great to get information to guide you through your life, but how do you interpret your dreams? You can always purchase a dream dictionary book or search for the information online. A dream dictionary gives you meaning of key things you dream about. For example if you dream about spiders it may indicate you feel disconnected from a situation like you are an outsider. Many things have more than one answer and while researching the content of your dream, read different meanings of the situation until you find one that relates to your life. I personally like to decode my own dreams, although it does take some time to connect the issues you are experiencing to your dream, but the more you do this the easier it will come.

One dream I had back a few years ago had significant meaning in my life regarding a person that I was working for at the time. It was truly an unhealthy relationship. This dream was recurring for me because my spirit guides were trying to assist me on making a difficult decision; to move on from the job regardless of the outcome that I was scared of. As soon as I made the connection and realized how this person was affecting me not only emotionally but also physically the dream stopped. I would like to share this dream with you. The dream is very long and vivid. Please visit www.ahigherenergy.net and click on the Dream Tab. Here you can read stories about dreams as well as blog about your own dreams.

The dream was about a witch that was in my home when I was having a gathering of all my friends. The witch was grabbing each one of my friends and sucking the life out of them literally and killing them.

This was the kind of dream that was so real and so vivid I would be scared when I woke up for a long time.

My lesson for the dream was opening doors to the unknown can bring an unwelcome reality into your life. Always yield with caution when indulging yourself into things you cannot control and have no knowledge about. When I finally understood this dream, my life took a giant turn towards a better future. I learned the importance of dreams and that I must pay attention to them. I hope you do the same. We as people are always searching for answers when they are right there within ourselves and play out for us as a movie every night. This dream was very intense at this time in my life. I was making decisions without really thinking and was starting to surround myself with people that devalued my life. They were needy and I believe now used me in order to bring me down. Misery loves company. This statement is very true. When people are unhappy in life they unknowingly will try to bring people down to a point lower than themselves in order to feel better. It took me some time to really figure this dream out, but it was this recurring dream that truly made me start my dream journal; mostly, because I wanted the dream to stop. The point was taken and I obviously was not getting the message so my guides presented me with a loud and clear message through my dreams. They would not stop until I figured it out, which I did. I did it by writing out my story and then reading it over and over again; relating it back to what was going on in my life. When you have a dream and you can make just one connection in how it relates to your life, all the other pieces of the dream begin to make sense.

I have developed a Dream Map that is very similar to your Life Map to help you in keeping track and decoding your own dreams. Here is an example of a blank Dream Map:

Description of your dream	How could it possibly fit into your life	Rules on your Mirror

I will review how to complete your Dream Map in the workbook section.

Meditation

Meditation is as easy or as hard as want to make it. I know the word meditation had always scared me a bit. I always felt like there is no way I can sit there in silence for any length of time with my mind blank. My mind is always running at 100 MPH hour thinking about everyone and everything you can image. I even fabricate some pretty strange day dreams in my mind as well. All of this all seems to go on in my mind at the same time. It is like a hurricane of thoughts constantly. I will say not much has changed for me in that area. I am a thinker and a daydreamer all rolled into one. When my Spirit Guides were nudging me in the direction of meditation I was just thinking "I Can't". Knowing that if I set the intention of "I can't" that is what will happen. I will not be able to meditate. So instead I said "I Can". I can meditate. So away I went, meditating away. Each and every time I tried I would constantly have things popping into my mind. When I was able to really relax I would just fall asleep. I knew that I had to find a balance between being able to relax, clearing my mind and meditation. Being the fighter I am I gave it my all. I am not a meditation expert at all. I am sharing with you, how I fit meditation into my life.

Meditation is being able to shut down your conscience mind and all the earthly thoughts that go along with it. Meditation is a great tool while working through this process. Meditation allows you to relax, reduce stress and receive knowledge from the Divine. I know for me I thought meditation was something you needed to do for an hour or so. I did a lot of reading and researching on how exactly you meditate. What I found was everyone does meditation differently. You must just figure out how you can do it and how meditation can fit into your life.

Meditation for me consists of about ten minutes a day. In these ten minutes I sit down in a comfortable chair and I just breathe and try to think of absolutely nothing. When a thought presents itself I push it away. As soon as I push that thought away, another one comes in. I just keep pushing all the thoughts that come in out of my mind. When I first began to meditate I spent the whole ten minutes just pushing thoughts away. If you find yourself doing the same thing, it is OK. Eventually through practice you will be able to shut your conscience mind off. By the act of pushing your thoughts away you are doing a lot for stress in your life. As those thoughts are coming in you are not continuously thinking about them, worrying about them and stressing over it. You do not allow yourself to because you are pushing the thought away.

Many of us on a daily basis have 1000 things we are responsible for and we are constantly thinking about what we have to do next. The 10 minutes of meditating will allow your mind to relax. Relaxing your mind, I know for me, has really helped with my stress level as well as with my ability to think clearer. I find it very helpful in my life.

Another way I also meditate is right before I fall asleep at night. This way when I do fall asleep it really is no big deal. I lie in my bed on my back and take deep breaths. As a thought enters, I push it away. I keep pushing my thoughts away until I begin to see colors. Once my mind is clear I can see colors that swirl around in my line of vision while my eyes are closed. These colors are what I concentrate on. What I watch before I go to sleep. Every night, without fail, I fall asleep without the tossing, turning and my mind running at 100 mph. You should try it.

How meditation fits into the process is because you need to be able to relax. You need to be able to clear your mind of all your worries and make decisions with your new found way of understanding yourself. If your mind is cluttered and you are feeling stressed you may make decisions that were not the best to make. Also, meditation is great in order to have your Spirit Guide help you through a problem. When a problem has surfaced that you really are struggling with you can meditate on it. I have heard this saying so much over my life and when people would say it I would chuckle to myself and laugh. Now I know what they mean. Meditating on something is wonderful. You can figure out your issue and make a decision so much easier and have faith the decision was correct. Your Spirit Guide will help you do this. Begin by having a paper and pen right next to you. Write out the situation you need to meditate on. Begin to meditate. As thoughts come into your mind push them away; all thoughts, even those that have to do with this situation. Keep pushing them away. Once your mind is clear think to yourself "OK I am ready for your help". Whatever thoughts you then have begin to write them all down. Just have the paper and pen next to you. Do not worry if you are writing it messy or not this is just for you.

Here are a few Ideas on how to fit ten minutes of meditation into your life.

Ten minutes is all you need:

- In the shower.

- At your desk at work.

- While you are using the bathroom.

- Right before you fall asleep.

- Right after you wake up.

- In your parked car before or after work.

- While the kids are napping, the chores can wait ten minutes.

It does not matter how you fit meditation into your life, just fit it in. The more you do meditation the better you will get at it and the easier it will be to do. I will go over some breathing exercises and meditation practices in the workbook section that assist you while meditating.

Signs

Your life journey is filled with signs to help guide you through your life. You just have to pay attention to them. It is natural for people to strive for things they want in life. Many of us fight and push our way to our goals we have set for ourselves without really taking a step back and analyzing if what we are fighting for is really worth it.

I have heard so many times recently that I am lucky. I am lucky because it seems to everyone else in my life that I get whatever it is I want. It is not that I get everything I want it is that I pay attention to the signs in my life that lead to what I should be receiving out of life. There are many things I want in life that I do not get because they just do not happen for me. The difference between me and some other people is I truly believe that if I do not get what I want there is a very good reason behind it. I do not dwell on the negative aspect of an outcome - I dwell on the positive.

Typically people notice the signs they should have followed once the decision they made did not work out to their benefit. You all know what I mean, I am sure most of you have said "I knew I should not have done this," or "I guess I should have paid attention when ….." Yes you should have paid attention. The reason why you didn't is because we are human and we are fighters. We know what we want and we keep pushing things until we get it. It is now time to stop pushing and begin to allow things to happen. I am not saying that you stop striving for things. I am saying you must stop pushing hard for things without really understanding how it is going to better your life.

Just like your Mirror and your Life Map the best way to start to notice signs in your life is to go over signs you have missed in the past. By going over the past you will see the trend of these signs. The more you understand how the signs had presented themselves in the past; you will be able to notice how the signs present themselves in the future.

To begin you must first start with a recent situation that you have gone through. I find it beneficial to begin with a situation you are already addressing on your life map. Once you know the situation I want you to answer the following questions and fill in the blanks.

What is the situation you would like to address on your Life Map?

_____

_____

_____

How did this situation affect your life?

_____

_____

_____

I should have known it was not going to end well when

_____

_____

_____

I should have paid attention when

_____

_____

_____

The signs you received were

_____

_____

_____

Go over this with all the situations you wrote about on your Life Map. The more you do this activity the better you will become at picking out signs as they are presented to you now.

Remember there is nothing you can do about the past, nothing at all. The past happened for a reason, a very important reason. You needed those experiences in order to learn your lesson and follow your life path. What you can control now is your future. You control your future by learning your lesson from your past experiences, setting positive intentions, following the guidance you receive everyday and utilizing the tools that are given to you.

Step Seven: New Beginning

How I truly believed in this process was by going through it and having faith that the guidance of my Spirit Guides was pointing me in the right direction. The more I followed the guidance the more things made sense. Things became clearer in my mind as to why I am the way I am. I began to see the connection of how all the bad things that happened in my life was because of how I viewed myself and other people. The more situations I reviewed, through the process of completing my life Map, the more times I could see the pattern of the same type of situations happening to me. I began to understand and appreciate my past experiences. I began to understand and appreciate the people that were part of those experiences in a whole new way. When I began to appreciate those individuals that I viewed before with hate and resentment, the lighter I began to feel. I began to feel lighter because I began to vibrate at "A Higher Energy". As I began to vibrate at "A higher Energy" I could see all the signs in my life that pointed me to my right path. As I began to live my life with this new understanding of myself and others, I also discovered what it is like to have true happiness; Happiness that is not easily sought by all. I am so grateful for this life of "A Higher Energy" and I thank my God and my

Spirit Guides every day. This New Beginning is what I hope and I pray for each and every one of you reading these pages. There may be times you think, "Yeah, Ok like this really going to work?" I am telling you it does. Read the book, do the activities and give yourself a chance at this New Beginning. If you find yourself slipping back to the negative mind set. Or just feeling heavy and sad, pick this book back up and read it again. I myself I have to do just that from time to time. I revisit everything I have learned and it kicks me right back to vibrating at "A Higher Energy".

Understanding You - Workbook

Step One: The Mirror

To begin the mirror process you must sit and begin to write everything down about yourself that you view as a flaw. Your flaws are the things that when you look in the mirror you see as a negative. Write down everything, your physical flaws, emotional flaws, personality flaws, ETC. All the things you have been holding on to that have contributed to your personal self-image.

As you begin this first step ask yourself the following statements and fill in the blanks:

   1. When I look in the mirror I see

_____

_____

_____

2. I have always been told that I

_____

_____

_____

_____?

3. I am constantly worrying about

_____

_____

_____

_____?

4. I am scared of

_____

_____

_____

5. I would make better decisions in my life, if I would stop

_____

_____

_____

_____?

6. My friends always told me I was

_____

_____

_____

_____?

7. My family always told me I was

_____

_____

_____

_____?

8. I believe my flaws are

_____

_____

_____

_____ ?

These questions will give you a great base to begin your mirror. As you complete your Life Map you will discover other rules you live your life by. As you discover other rules just add them to your mirror.

Humor Cures all   **Smart**   **I Hate my self**

People are mean

Life is not fair

I talk too much

I talk too much   ***Never say no***

I deserve abuse

I am dirty   I am fat

I am ugly

I have greasy hair

food makes me feel better

Self centered   Trust no one

People think, I think I am better

As you begin to answer the questions and write down all the negative rules on your mirror keep them in a journal or in the following blank pages of this book. The act of writing down your negative rules, that you are becoming more and more aware of, is taking ownership of them.

Many rules you discover will be things that you may never want to admit to anyone. Which, I can completely understand. Now is the time for you to admit it to yourself and take ownership of the rule and begin to change the rule. Every Person who begins this process finds a personal journal a very key tool to the program. Another method of journaling your thoughts is through blogging. Please visit www.ahigherenergy.net and go to the "The Mirror" tab on the site. Useful documents are listed there as well as a blog. The blog can be your personal journal. When registering for the blog simply use a sign in ID that will make you be anonymous.

The Mirror (Notes)

The Mirror (Notes)

_____

_____

_____

_____

_____

_____

_____

_____

_____

_____

_____

_____

_____

_____

_____

_____

_____

Stacy-Lynn

The Mirror (Notes)

_____

_____

_____

_____

_____

_____

_____

_____

_____

_____

_____

_____

_____

_____

_____

_____

Step Two: Life Map

You will want to begin by filling in each part of the chart. You can begin with whatever situation that comes to mind first. The chart is divided into 7 columns. Here are the descriptions of each column:

Age: The approximate age you were when the situation occurred.

Experience – Personal Relationships: Complete if the situation had to do with your personal relationships. Personal relationships include family members, Spouses, Boyfriends and Girlfriends.

Experience – Friendships: Complete if the situation had to do with Friends or acquaintances.

Experience – Work: Complete if the situation had to with your career.

Experience – Yourself: Complete if the situation is about things you have done or are doing to yourself.

Rules: What rules on your mirror contributed to getting into this situation? What rules on your mirror were created because of this situation?

Person: What person or people did this situation involve?

Age	Experience - Personal Relationships	Experience - Friendships	Experience - Work	Experience - Your Self	Rules	People

Step One of the Life Map: It is best if you go to <u>www.ahigherenergy.net</u> and click of the Life Map Tab. Download the excel spreadsheet labeled Life Map. This will allow you to have a larger version of the life map.

Step Two of the Life Map: Pick a rule on your mirror and ask yourself, "When was the last time this rule affected my life negatively?" Write in your life map under the **Rule** column the rule you are referring too. Then under the appropriate column write a brief explanation about the event.

Step Three of the Life Map: Under the Person column write down the people that were involved in the event including yourself, this is beginning the list of those you need to forgive.

Step Four of the Life Map: Under the Age column complete the age in which you were when the event happened.

Step Five of the Life Map: Ask yourself, "Due to this situation what other rules were either created or reinforced. Write that rule under the Rule column. Continue with this until you have gone back far enough to see the bridge to your past and how it is connected to your present self. Are you convinced that this rule needs to be changed? If so continue with the next rule. Make sure you write down all the new rules you discover through the process of completing your Life Map on your negative Mirror.

Another very effective way is to journal your stories. Many people like to write out the experiences in full detail. That is great if you prefer that. Just ensure you are still keeping notes to the rules you need to change and the people you need to forgive. You can also Blog your journal at www.ahigherenergy.net. Click on the Life Map Tab and go into the blog. The blog is a great tool that you can express you fears and concerns over this process and received comments from everyone who is going through the same thing. I myself use this blog.

Life Map (notes)

_____

_____

_____

_____

_____

_____

_____

_____

_____

_____

_____

_____

_____

_____

_____

Life Map (notes)

_____

_____

_____

_____

_____

_____

_____

_____

_____

_____

_____

_____

_____

_____

_____

_____

Life Map (notes)

_____

_____

_____

_____

_____

_____

_____

_____

_____

_____

_____

_____

_____

_____

_____

_____

Step Three: Intentions

To begin the process of setting positive intentions in your life you must first create a new positive mirror of rules. In Step One: The Mirror you discovered what negative rules are on your mirror. Some of my negative rules were:

I am fat, I have Greasy Hair, I am Dirty, Talk too much, Self Centered, People think I think I am better than them, Smart, I deserve abuse, I hate myself, Humor cures all, Food always makes you feel better, never say No, trust no one, people are mean, life is not fair, I am ugly, sex makes me sick

Now that you know some of your negative rules, you can begin to recreate new positive rules to live your life by. How you create new rules in your life, is by writing down all of the negative rules that were placed on your mirror. Ensure to include all the rules you wrote down on your Mirror in step one and the rules you discovered through your Life Map under the Rule column. Next to each negative rule, write something positive about yourself. Here is how mine looks:

- I am fat – I am beautiful

- I have Greasy Hair - Blonde Beautiful Curls

- I am Dirty – Clean

- Talk too much – I love a good conversation

- Self Centered – I care about people

- People think I think I am better than them – My life is great and I deserve it

- Smart – Smart

- I deserve abuse – No one abuses me

- I hate myself – I love myself

- Humor cures all – I am not a joke

- Food always makes you feel better – I make myself feel better

- Never say No – I do what is best for me

- Trust no one – trust those that can be trusted

- People are mean – Everyone has their own Life Map

- Life is not fair – Life is what you make it

- I am ugly – I am pretty

- Sex makes me sick – I am safe

Now that you know what your new rules will be, you need to remind yourself of them every day.

How you do that is by creating a reminder for yourself. Take all the positive rules and create a new mirror. You create this new mirror just simply by creating a picture out of all the new rules or just by simply listing all the new rules on a piece of paper. You can be as creative as you want with your new rules just make sure that you post this new mirror in your home next to some type of real mirror. You do this so you will see your new rules every day. You place them by a real mirror in your home so every day you can look in the mirror while you read these new rules to yourself. Take the time everyday to recite these rules to yourself. This step is very important. Remember your negative rules were reinforced to you over and over again through actions of other people and through your own actions. That constant reminder is what made those negative rules, the rules you live by. You now need that constant reminder of your new positive rules. Recite your rules to yourself every time you look in the mirror. Memorize your new rules and say them to yourself in your mind throughout your day. You may even want to write some of the rules on a small piece of paper that you can keep with you. Whenever you notice your mind wandering back to negative and unproductive thoughts you must recite your new positive rules.

I am not a joke   Smart   *Blonde beautiful curls*

My life is great, I deserve it

Trust those that can be trusted   *I do what is best for me*

Clean   Life is what you make it

I make myself feel better

I love a good conversation

No one abuses me

Everyone has their own Life Map

I am safe

I am beautiful

I LOVE myself

I care about people

Intentions (notes)

_____

_____

_____

_____

_____

_____

_____

_____

_____

_____

_____

_____

_____

_____

_____

_____

_____

Stacy-Lynn

Intentions (notes)

_____

_____

_____

_____

_____

_____

_____

_____

_____

_____

_____

_____

_____

_____

_____

_____

_____

Stacy-Lynn

Intentions (notes)

_____

_____

_____

_____

_____

_____

_____

_____

_____

_____

_____

_____

_____

_____

_____

_____

Step Four: Forgiveness

When I began going through this process forgiveness was easy for me. It was easy once I truly believed in myself and believed that everyone is living their own life while learning their own life lessons.

Here are the steps to take in order to forgive:

Step One: You must first identify who in your life you need to forgive. While completing your life Map you wrote down in the "People" column the individuals that were part of that situation. These are the people you need to forgive.

Step Two: Select a person from your life Map to begin with. Write that individual name down on a piece of paper. Next to their Name I want you to write "I forgive you". You must begin by setting the intention of I will forgive. Believe this intention.

Step three: Think about how this person has affected your life. Write down all the rules on your mirror that this person either set for you or reinforced for you.

Step Four: Write down all the things that you know happened to this person in their life that influenced who they are. What you are doing is recreating a small version of their Life Map.

Step Five: If you do not know this person write down what you think could have happened to them in order to be the person they are that was able to do those things to you.

Step Six: Imagine this person as a child. Read all the thing you either know or think happened to them in their life.

Step Seven: Turn your hate and resentment into pity for them.

By taking the time to think about this person and all the rules they have on their mirror will give you a better understanding as to why they are the way they are; just like you did for yourself. You have got to believe that every person is living their life they are meant to live. That all of us are all intermingled together living our lives through the bad times and the good. Remember that we all have to experience the bad in order to learn our lessons. In order to experience the bad other people need to be part of it. So whether you were the one doing the bad things or the victim of someone else, it all happened for reason. Regardless of how horrible the experience was you must look at the big picture, learn your lesson and let go of the hate and resentment that you developed from it.

Forgiveness for me was easy because I believed I could do it and I believed in this entire process. If forgiveness is difficult for you, that is OK. Continue on with the process. The more you go through the process, you will see all the good in your life and how you can truly be a leader of it, the forgiveness will become easy.

Forgiveness (notes)

_____

_____

_____

_____

_____

_____

_____

_____

_____

_____

_____

_____

_____

_____

_____

_____

_____

_____

Stacy-Lynn

Forgiveness (notes)

_____

_____

_____

_____

_____

_____

_____

_____

_____

_____

_____

_____

_____

_____

_____

_____

_____

Stacy-Lynn

Forgiveness (notes)

Stacy-Lynn

Step Five: Spirit Guide

I believe the best way to begin a relationship is through a guided mediation. Please visit www.ahigherenergy.net and click on the Understanding You Tab Step Five: Spirit Guide to download the below guided meditation. Before you begin your meditation have a pen and paper ready, to journal all that you saw, felt, heard or just knew. Describe your Spirit Guide. Did they tell you their name? Are they a man or women? What did they look like, feel like or sound like? Whatever information you received write it down. The first time that you do this guided mediation you may only get a small piece of information. The more you do this meditation the more information you will get. Just ensure that you always journal all of the information you do receive so that you can always have your notes to refer back to.

Spirit Guides really are an important part of each and every one of our lives. They have been with us since the moment we were born. They have walked next to us for years without a voice or even and acknowledgement from us for all of their hard work. Your Spirit Guides want you to know they are there. They want us to use them as much as possible when making decisions throughout our lives. You can use the meditation to begin a line of communication with your guide but you can also just believe they are there. Talk to your guides, ask their advice and then just listen to thoughts that come into your mind. Your Spirit Guides also help guide you by pointing out signs for you to follow. You will become better at noticing and following those signs the more you work through this process.

When I began to consciously work with my Spirit Guide I selected a sign for them. I knew whenever I saw my sign, it was my Spirit Guide just saying, "Yes, I am with you". My sign I selected was lady bugs. I still use this sign today. It is amazing especially when I am going through a difficult time I see lady bugs everywhere, even in the middle of winter. Take a moment and select a sign for your Spirit Guide and watch as it pops up all over the place. One more thing, always make sure you thank your Spirit Guide!

Spirit Guide Meditation

Take a deep breath through your nose and hold it 1….2….3…. and let it our through your mouth. Let all of the air in your lungs out hold it 1….2….3…….

Take a deep breath through your nose and hold it 1….2….3…. and let it our through your mouth. Let all of the air in your lungs out hold it 1….2….3…….

Take a deep breath through your nose and hold it 1….2….3…. and let it our through your mouth. Let all of the air in your lungs out hold it 1….2….3…….

Begin to breathe normally with your eyes closed every time you hear your breath coming in to your lungs and then out you become more and more relaxed.

In and out.......in and out........in and out.........

You are standing in the middle of a dirt road and you begin to walk down the road you see on you right side a path that leads through a small field. Take that path...

As you are walking through the small field you notice the path turns slightly to the left..........

Continue walking on the path..................

The sun is bright but the weather is cool. You hear so many wonderful noises. You here a hawk and look up to him in flight over the field........

As you continue on your path you notice that the path leads into the woods..........

Continue on your path...........

As you are walking down the path through the woods you look up and admire the beauty of the leaves they are starting to turn to so many shades of orange.........yellow..........red............

You take a deep breath you can smell autumn in the air a small breeze blows and it gives a bit of goose bumps on your arms.

Listen to the noises of nature.......... birds chirping........... Ruffling of leaves...........scratching of branches...............

You see a small chipmunk run across the path just up in front of you...............

Continue down the path............

You start to notice you are beginning to descend......

You are now walking down a hill......

The hill is very easy to walk down. You feel very safe and know that you will not fall.....

The closer you get to the bottom of the hill the trees start to thin.......

You begin to notice sand beneath your feet......

You can hear waves.........

As you come to the bottom of the hill to you emerge on to a beach.........

Walk along the beach......................

It is a beautiful day..........

As you are walking down the beach you see there is a small hut right up in front of you........

Go to the hut.........

The hut is empty.....

Sit down on the sand in the middle of the hut and close your eyes...........

You can hear yourself breath and you feel the rays of sun coming through the holes on the roof.

Keep your eyes closed..........breathing in and out

You feel someone enter the hut with you keep your eyes closed.......

You feel them sit down in front of you.......

Reach out your hand and allow them to take it……..

Open your eyes………This is your Spirit Guide…..

Is your guide a man or women……what do they look like……. Take some time with your guide talk with them……

Walk with them back up the hill and allow them to guide you back while you talk. Take as much time as you need.

Now you have created a sacred place for you and your guide. You can visit this beach side hut whenever you would like to communicate directly with your Spirit Guides.

Spirit Guide (notes)

Spirit Guide (notes)

_____

_____

_____

_____

_____

_____

_____

_____

_____

_____

_____

_____

_____

_____

_____

_____

Spirit Guide (notes)

Step Six: Dream Interpretation, Meditation and Signs

Dream Interpretation

When you first begin to interpret your own dreams I find it beneficial to use a dream Map I have created as well as a dream journal. Here is an example of a blank Dream Map.

Description of your dream	How could it possibly fit into your life	Rules on your Mirror

The Dream map is very simply and straight forward. It is divided into three columns.

Description of your dream: Write a brief description of what your dream was about. List everything you saw in your dream, even if you think it may not be relevant.

How could it possibly fit into your life?: Use this column to write down everything you can think of that is going on in your life that could pertain to your dream. For example if you are dreaming that you are running away from something then think about what in your life are you either hiding from or running away from. Is there a major decision in your life that you need to make but you are avoiding it? Are you having problems in your personal relationships that you just do not want to admit? Here is where you really need to take a moment and think outside the box a bit. Keep in mind the more you do this activity of completing the Dream Map the easier it will be to interpret your own dreams.

Rules on you mirror: Use this column to write down the rules on your mirror that may be playing a role as to why you are having this dream. For example if you are dreaming about your teeth falling out then you may have a rule on your mirror that you are unhappy with your physical appearance. If you are dreaming about being unfaithful in your relationship you may have a rule on your mirror in regards to trust. Take this time to really think about what rules on my mirror could fit into the topic of your dream. The more you do this activity the easier it will be to interpret your own dreams. You then can use your skills in helping other people interpret their dreams as well.

Dreams (notes)

_____

_____

_____

_____

_____

_____

_____

_____

_____

_____

_____

_____

_____

_____

_____

_____

_____

_____

_____

Dreams (notes)

_____

_____

_____

_____

_____

_____

_____

_____

_____

_____

_____

_____

_____

_____

_____

_____

Dreams (notes)

Stacy-Lynn

Meditation

Meditation is as easy or hard as you would like it to be. I want to review with you the steps I have taken in order to fit mediation into my life. The meditation techniques that I use are very basic. If you would like more information on mediation please visit my site www.ahigherenergy.net . There are useful links to sites and books that will help you in developing your meditation techniques.

Here are the steps I follow when I begin to meditate.

Step one: You want to find a quite comfortable place where you will not be disturbed for at least ten minutes. This may be in your home, office, car or even the bathroom.

Step Two: Sit down comfortably with your hands in front of you on your lap or on the arm rests of a chair. I find it more beneficial to sit comfortable then lay down. This is because if I am lying down I am more likely to fall asleep.

Step Three: Breathe deeply in through your nose and out of your mouth. Hold your Breath each time for a count of three.

Breathe in through your nose….. Hold it for 1……2……3…..

Breathe out of your mouth......Hold it for 1.....2......3........

When you breathe in, breathe in as much air as you can. Fill your lungs up completely or as much as you can. When you breathe out ensure that you are pushing all the air out of your lungs or as much as you can. Continue this breathing for a minute or two and then begin breathing at you normal pace.

Step Three: Breathe in and breathe out. With each breath you breathe in picture the air you breathe as a beautiful white light. When you breathe the air out envision that air as filled with all the worries and stress you have leaving your body.

Breathe in beautiful white light. Breathe out all your stress and frustration.

Breathe in beautiful white light. Breathe out all your stress and frustration.

Do this breathing the entire ten minutes or as long as you are able to meditate.

Step Four: Continue with your breathing and as thoughts enter your mind, push them away. You will catch yourself running with a thought, that is ok, just as soon as you realize it just push it away and begin to concentrate on your breathing again.

Breathe in beautiful white light. Breathe out all your stress and frustration.

Step Five: Keep pushing away your thought until you mind is calm and clear. You may spend the whole time you are mediating pushing away thoughts that is OK, just keep doing it.

Getting to the point of a completely calm and clear mind is definitely not an easy task. Some of you may try it once and think how easy it is and some may always spend their time pushing away thoughts. However you respond to meditation is perfect.

Here are a few Ideas on how to fit ten minutes of meditation into your life.

Ten minutes is all you need:

- In the shower.

- At your desk at work.

- While you are using the bathroom.

- Right before you fall asleep.

- Right after you wake up.

- In your parked car before or after work.

- While the kids are napping, the chores can wait ten minutes.

It does not matter how you fit meditation into your life, just fit it in. The more you do meditation the better you will get at it and the easier it will be to do.

Another way I also meditate is right before I fall asleep at night. This way when I do fall asleep it really is no big deal. I lie in my bed on my back and take deep breaths. As a thought enters, I push it away. I keep pushing my thoughts away until I begin to see colors. Once my mind is clear I can see colors that swirl around in my line of vision while my eyes are closed. These colors are what I concentrate on. What I watch before I go to sleep. Every night, without fail, I fall asleep without the tossing, turning and my mind running at 100 mph. You should try it.

You can also use meditation to work with your Spirit Guides. Your Spirit Guides are with you to assist you throughout your lives and you can use mediation to work more consciously with your Spirit Guides.

Here are the steps I follow when I use meditation to get assistance from my Spirit Guide.

Step One: Get a pen and paper and on the top of the paper write down what it is that you would like guidance from your Spirit Guide on.

Step Two: You want to find a quite comfortable place where you will not be disturbed. In order to write down all the information that comes into your mind, you will want to sit comfortably at a table. That can be at a desk, kitchen table or anywhere, where you can set you paper down and be able to write comfortable without interruption. .

Step Three: Begin your breathing exercises again. Breathe deeply in through your nose and out of your mouth. Hold your Breath each time for a count of three.

Breathe in through your nose….. Hold it for 1……2……3…..

Breathe out of your mouth……Hold it for 1…..2……3……..

When you breathe in, breathe in as much air as you can. Fill your lungs up completely or as much as you can. When you breathe out ensure that you are pushing all the air out of your lungs or as much as you can. Continue this breathing for a minute or two and then begin breathing at your normal pace.

Step Three: Breathe in and breathe out. With each breath you breathe in picture the air you breathe as a beautiful white light. When you breathe the air out envision that air as filled with all the worries and stress you have leaving your body.

Breathe in beautiful white light. Breathe out all your stress and frustration.

Breathe in beautiful white light. Breathe out all your stress and frustration.

Step Four: Continue with your breathing and as thoughts enter your mind, push them away. You will catch yourself running with a thought, that is ok, just as soon as you realize it just push it away and begin to concentrate on your breathing again.

Breathe in beautiful white light. Breathe out all your stress and frustration.

Step Five: Keep pushing away your thoughts until you mind is calm and clear. Once your mind is clear recite either out loud or within your mind what you would like guidance on from your Spirit Guide. Then begin to write all the thoughts that come into your mind.

The guidance will seem as though it is your own thoughts. Some people may hear the guidance in the form of voices within their heads. Some people see flashes of pictures or just know what it is that is being told to them. Whichever way you get the information is Ok just write down all that you either hear, feel, see or just know.

As with anything new you begin to do practice is what will make you better. My biggest advice is to not second guess what you should write. Write down everything. Things will become clearer the more you do this activity. I do want to tell you that whenever you receive guidance from you Spirit Guides it will always be positive. They would never guide you to do things that are not in the best interest of you or other people. Your Spirit Guides are Divine in every way, shape and form. If your thoughts are negative and hurtful then it is not guidance from your Spirit Guides.

Meditation (notes)

Meditation (notes)

Meditation (notes)

_____

_____

_____

_____

_____

_____

_____

_____

_____

_____

_____

_____

_____

_____

_____

_____

Signs

Just like your Mirror and your Life Map the best way to start to notice signs in your life is to go over signs you have missed in the past. By going over the past you will see the trend of these signs. The more you understand how the signs had presented themselves in the past you will be able to notice how the signs present themselves in the future.

To begin you must first start with a recent situation that you have gone through. I find it beneficial to begin with a situation you are already addressing on your life map. Once you know the situation I want you to answer the following questions and fill in the blanks.

What is the situation you would like to address on your Life Map?

_____

_____

_____

How did this situation affect your life?

_____

_____

_____

I should have known it was not going to end well when

_____

_____

_____

_____

I should have paid attention when

_____

_____

_____

_____

The signs you received were

_____

_____

_____

_____

Go over this with all the situations you wrote about on your Life Map. The more you do this activity the better you will become at picking out signs as they are presented to you now.

Remember there is nothing you can do about the past, nothing at all. The past happen for a reason, a very important reason. You needed those experiences in order to learn your lesson and follow your life path. What you can control now is your future. You control you future by learning your lesson from your past experiences, setting positive intentions, following the guidance you receive everyday and utilizing the tools that are given to you.

Signs (notes)

_____

_____

_____

_____

_____

_____

_____

_____

_____

_____

_____

_____

_____

_____

_____

Signs (notes)

_____

_____

_____

_____

_____

_____

_____

_____

_____

_____

_____

_____

_____

_____

_____

_____

Signs (notes)

_____

_____

_____

_____

_____

_____

_____

_____

_____

_____

_____

_____

_____

_____

_____

_____

Step Seven: New Beginning

Change is never easy and especially changing your frame of mind. If you follow each step of the Understanding You Process and truly dedicate the time for yourself you will see a vast improvement in your life.

Just some helpful reminders:

- Remember you are not alone.

- Visit www.ahigherenergy.net and use the tools that are available to you.

- Read the blog.

- Give advice to other people as well as accept advice from them.

- Start a journal. The act of writing things down that you are working on is a way to release them.

- Do the activities in this workbook. Actually going through the steps will help.

- Remind yourself of your new positive intentions.

- Read your new rules on your mirror.

- Believe in yourself

- Allow yourself to live a life vibrating at "A Higher Energy"

New Beginning (notes)

_____

_____

_____

_____

_____

_____

_____

_____

_____

_____

_____

_____

_____

_____

_____

_____

Stacy-Lynn

New Beginning (notes)

New Beginning (notes)

New Beginning (notes)

_____

_____

_____

_____

_____

_____

_____

_____

_____

_____

_____

_____

_____

_____

_____

_____

_____